The Art of Manifestation:

Simple Energy Techniques to Create the Abundant Life You Deserve

By Rev. Mignon Grayson
Sacred Mysteries World Wide, LLC

The Art of Manifestation:
Simple Energy Techniques to Create the
Abundant Life You Deserve

Rev. Mignon Grayson

Copyright 2019
United States Copyright Office

DEDICATION

This book is dedicated to Olodumare / Ntr / God, my Ancestors, my Spirit Guides, my spiritual Elders, and to Onile (earth) for the life and inspiration that flows through me. This book is gift from them. May I always continue to receive their blessings as I walk upon this earth.

This book is also dedicated to You, the Reader. May you discover the beauty, uniqueness and power of your Spirit and realize your ultimate potential and ability to co-create your life with the Creator.

MANIFESTATION
INVOCATION

I see my dream in its tangible form.

I hear the way it sounds.

I feel the way it makes my heartbeat.

My vision for its fulfillment is complete.

And now, I align myself and this deepest desire

with the good of all things, and the great knowing of the Universe.

I release my dream into the matrix, holding fast to the vision.

I freefall into trust. It will happen. It is happening. It is here.

I awaken my Root for the strength to endure.

I summon my passion to create and give birth.

I summon my inner will to push through.

I call to my Guides for insight.

I take action, I do the work, and then I am patient.

I release what does not serve me

to make way for my dream, the good it will bring,

and the space it will require in my life.

Amen, Asé, Aho, and So it is.

The Goal of this Book

The goal of this book is to present to the reader various methods and tools of manifestation that can be used effectively. The information presented in this book can be used in whole or in part. Through the coming pages discover what resonates with you and stay with the process. Not all of these manifestation techniques are for everybody. The important thing is to find what works for you. As with all things that are to be accomplished, consistency is an important factor. Stay with the techniques you can be consistent with. Use one, some, or all. It's entirely up to you. It's your life. Now, go and claim what you want!

The reason you are reading this book on manifestation is because you believe that it is possible for people to manifest on purpose. You are aware of the unseen vibratory reality that supports all of life. You also know that there is a Divine Creator, God, Goddess, Great Spirit, Universe that is the source of all creation. You also know that you are made in the likeness of this Creator and are, therefore, Divine and capable of creation. These are the fundamental truths that you must know in order for the techniques in this book to work for you.

Manifestation is the process by which you utilize the realm of potentiality along with physical, mental, emotional and energetic tools in order to affect changes and to acquire desired things or circumstances. This can be accomplished through applying the techniques in this book.

The process of manifesting your desires will also help you to connect with your Higher Self and own your personal power more profoundly. This is emotionally and mentally liberating and will help you to elevate your consciousness and grow spiritually.

1

Energy & Vibration

First, there needs to be an awareness and understanding that everything is vibration. All things vibrate at varying rates/resonances. The vibrational energy of the things (physical and non-physical) you want can be matched to align your personal vibration to it. Aligning your personal vibration will harmonize and magnify the attraction of it to you. Within the coming pages you will be introduced to several ways to do this. Although the mechanics may differ, the principles upon which they operate are the same. In this book the words energy, frequency, vibration, and resonance, refer to different states of the same source -- Primordial Source or Primordial Force. It is from this core energetic force that all manifestation originates. Everything is made from the primordial source which means all uncreated and created life (animate and inanimate) has consciousness because it originates from this primordial source.

As humans, we can access this source through our own focused intent and energy. It takes commitment, consistency, repetition and discipline. You have the ability. It only takes a decision and implementation of various techniques shared in this book.

The art of manifesting is a creative process involving the world of energy and vibration. There are many different approaches to how to energetically create your abundant life. This book is one way to open yourself up to discovering the vast theories and practices that are available.

Potentiality & the Gateway of Manifestation

Our inner potential makes us who we are as humans. It is always just beneath the surface for us to tap into to manifest our desires. It is this potential that is the force all of life draws upon to manifest. It is also responsible for our ability to continuously exceed top performance levels in every area of life. It is the root power of manifestation.

An obvious example is in the world of sports when athletes continue to exceed beyond the world records, setting new ones. Athletes are continuously excelling beyond what was previously the highest performance level. The realm of potential is a crucial part of how these breakthroughs happen. With a strong desire, mindset, training, and visualization athletes are able to access this realm of potential to accomplish their goals. They do it instinctively, for the most part. You don't have to know about it to access it. We were all born with the instinct to tap into this power.

Human potential exists at a level that is called "mind level." However, potentiality is all around us in the galaxy and in all of life (seen and unseen). Everything that has ever existed in the world existed first in the formless realm of potentiality. Like gravity. It is a force that is of great importance to existence, but it is not visible. There is immense power in it.

Most of us unconsciously draw from this realm of potentiality throughout our lifetime. For the purpose of intentional manifestation, we can consciously connect with this realm to create the life we desire and deserve. There is an inner access point, a gateway, where potential meets manifestation. This is the point where we can bring things or conditions into being.

Your Personal Energetic Signature

All human beings are incarnated into this world as spiritual beings housed in physical bodies. Your spirit and physical body work together to resonate your own unique vibrational energy. This is your core energy. Your "home" energy. Your soul energy. This is the energetic frequency that makes you unique. The is the frequency that is your personality. As you move through life, your personal vibrational energy goes through slight changes. It all depends on the interplay between your thoughts (conscious and subconscious), emotions, and actions. These fluctuations happen all the time due to environment and life experiences. You know how you can feel "off" some days and not quite yourself, a little down? Equally, your energy fluctuations occur when you are extremely uplifted and excited about how your life is going. In either example, your personal vibrational energy can fluctuate from exposure to positive or negative internal or external influences. Another example of this is how you sense someone else seems different to you than perhaps the day before. That is because their personal energy is fluctuating and vibrating slightly differently due to influences that effect their personal vibration. Your frequency vacillates according to what you are doing, thinking and feeling, but there is a core energetic "You" that remains constant. Take the element of water for example. Water is made up certain components that make it water. When you apply heat to it at some point it starts to boil, but it is still water. Once you remove the heat, it returns back to its original state. Your emotions and thoughts affect your vibration in a similar way. Emotional, intellectual and energetic circumstances act as catalysts for your personal energy to fluctuate and temporarily change. But you are you, no matter the fluctuations. The great news is that you can control and modify the fluctuations. The first step is being aware. The next step is learning the techniques that will empower you, such as meditation, concentration, visualization, and breathing patterns (pranayama.)

Your Thoughts Form Your Reality

We are thinking machines. That is what we do all day and all night, even when we are asleep. Thoughts are also energy. Thoughts can become form. Everything that is in your life and in the world is the result of thoughts. Your life is a combination of the all the thoughts that you have accepted and acted upon. The good thing is, we can change how we think to be in alignment with what we desire and bring those desires into manifestation.

The art of manifestation is the ability to utilize your personal energy and the energy around you and change it in ways that bring your desires into your life. Your personal energetic vibration (spiritual), your thoughts (mental), your actions (physical) and align them all to be in harmony with the vibration of the life you want to have and the things you want to acquire. As simple as it may sound, it takes work. It takes being fully committed to the process. It takes being aware all of the time of how you are thinking and what you are doing. Your subconscious will need to be accessed and nurtured with thoughts that support your intentions, as well. However, your subconscious is not as easily accessible to influence, but it can be through a technique I call "minding the subconscious" which uses methods to access and imprint on your subconscious. Minding the subconscious is, basically, using self-hypnosis and subliminal suggestion techniques.

Manifesting your desires takes utilizing all of the available tools that will support your manifestation goals. Additionally, incorporating extended focus and concentration, strong intent and elimination of distractions are also some of what is required.

My Personal Manifestation Story

When I began the process of manifesting a half a million dollars in 2016, I applied the manifestation techniques that I knew at the time. Since then, my journey of manifestation has taught me new techniques and deepened the techniques that I already knew. It brought new insights that I wanted to share with others. Here is my story...

I knew I had to produce more money in order to move myself out of my job and on my way to my passion, my life's work. I had NO idea how. But I just KNEW I had to do something. It was this burning desire that would drive me towards manifesting over $500,000 within a year.

Back in 2016 at the end of the year... around November/December a thought popped in my head as I began to contemplate the coming new year. Looking back at it now, I can say with certainty I was spiritually led to do this action. I took an index card and a black tip sharpie pen and wrote out the amount of money I wanted to manifest in the coming year on it. I didn't realize at the time, but I had set wheels firmly in motion by that simple act. I later learned this is called "Manifestation Scripting."

First and really important in abundance thinking, is a strong desire for something. For me it was to be out of the job I was in but financially ok. I wanted to have my own business and devote time and energy in the spiritual and creative fields—music in particular. "Spirit and Creativity," had been and is my theme in life. I so desperately wanted to change fields and be able to spend my time doing and being that which brings me much more satisfaction and joy. I made up my mind! I had decided to create this change in my life by increasing the flow of money using abundance techniques, how much did I think I could manifest? I settled on $500,000. It felt right. So, I took 3 index cards and wrote boldly on each one $500,000. I placed two of them in my wallet in two different places so that I would run into them frequently to remind me as a form of subliminal suggestion. The third one was placed inside my bowl of crystals on the table beside my bed to act as enhancers and magnifiers. Crystals are from the earth and represent abundance as well as have specific energies that are potent within them. By my beside was another location I knew I would repeatedly see it over and over again. This is subliminal programming of my subconscious. I listened to uplifting abundance and success speakers every morning, as well as used self-hypnosis techniques every day. I did daily visualization and recited affirmations. I also solicited the assistance of my spirit guides and ancestors gaining their support and help. They exist in the spirit realm which is another energetic dimension. They have the ability to remove energy blockages that may be in the way, as well as provide guidance, insight and inspiration for the best actions to take next.

What happened later in the year and throughout 2017 was amazing. I was able to leave my job with a package because they were doing a mass layoff. I was able to put my position in for consideration and it was accepted. The company was offering double the time of what my position would normally get, plus benefits. I was able to get my full salary and medical coverage for me and daughter for 9 months. This package totaled about $90,000. I was able to leave the job I wanted to leave with a juicy package that supported myself and my daughter for 9 straight months.

Didn't work for a penny of it. Toward the end of the 9 months, I again, was able to negotiate another settlement deal with my landlord at the time to buy me out of my rent-controlled apartment for $425,000. This was a great deal because I already owned a home not far away and could move into one of the three apartments. (The acquisition of this home is another manifestation story for another time.)

I aligned my personal energy to what I wanted to achieve by using a few of the manifestation techniques in this book. People who are successful do this all the time in one form or another. Many, I can guess, do it by instinct and not necessarily by a specific manifestation plan. When we are aware of the mechanics of manifestation, it can be applied with intention.

Upon reflection, I have noticed that when I absolutely knew that I would not accept anything other than a particular outcome, it happened very much in line with how I thought it to be. It was only when I faltered and allowed my ego (showing up as insecurity, doubt and fear) to take hold, did things not turn out the way I wanted. We are in constant co-creation with the Divine/the Universe. Usually, when I was certain of how I wanted the outcome to be and unaccepting of anything else, it was due to a "do or die" situation. An emergency. When it was something that I wanted, but was insecure about or felt unworthy, that is when the outcome was less in my favor or not at all. Mindset and unwavering knowing are extremely important.

You Are Already Manifesting

Truth is, we are all born Manifestors. You are already manifesting each and every day. You are using some of the techniques in this book already, albeit, unknowingly. That is what got you where you are right here and now. What you want to do, going forward, is manifest on purpose.

Take a moment to mentally review your day yesterday. For most of us, we woke up, got out of bed and began the day -- whether it was taking a shower/bath, drinking tea/coffee, eating breakfast, doing your makeup, grooming, putting on clothes, walking out the door and proceeding to your job and arriving there. Entering the building and beginning the workday. In your mind right now, you can see everything that happened with certainty and clarity. These are important elements in manifesting.

Ok, so let's look at this scenario from a manifestation perspective. You, by your sheer intention followed by your actions, went through your entire morning routine to get yourself to your job. The night before you probably prepped physically or mentally. In this regard, you sent confirmation to your subconscious of how the morning would go. These internal conversations and imagery that go on inside your mind are the things that fuel manifestation. You decided and confirmed (mental conversation & imagery) exactly how your morning would go. You envisioned it. You internally confirmed and reconfirmed it with yourself inside of your mind. When the morning came, you executed it. This is a level of manifestation that "happens" to everyone daily. Emphasis on "happens" is because most people are unaware. You have already incorporated several of the manifestation techniques such as: putting your ENERGY into a BELIEF in something that you are going to do. You projected your mind there (MENTAL/THOUGHTS). You planned it out (INTENTIONS). You VISUALIZED it, which made it even more concrete. You KNEW with CERTAINTY that your morning would play out the way it did... and it did.

As you go about your day-to-day, you are investing in your current series of activities. You are feeding it with your Will and powering it up with your personal vibrational energy. With your energy, you are continuously confirming it as your current reality – as the truth of your life. Mentally, you are replaying in your mind the script that you've accepted to live by. You absolutely could have decided that, "tomorrow I will not get up. I will not get ready. I will not go to work." You could have decided to do things differently.

Another example is to think back to when you had an emergency situation that required a solution by a certain time. Take a moment to reflect on how much mental and emotional energy you poured into solving the issue. How extended your concentration was until you either decided on a course of action or some type of solution was brought to you (MAGNETIZED). This is the stuff that powers manifestation! These are the elements to incorporate into your intentional manifestation work. The "secret sauce" so to speak. You are already doing it. Now it's time to take control and direct it.

In intentional manifesting, the element that is tricky is that you have no proof because you haven't experienced what you are desiring yet. There is no concrete confirmation that what you are desiring is going to manifest. You, as a Manifestor, will need to infuse your work with unwavering belief, better yet, a "knowingness" that when you engage in manifestation techniques it will work. This is where your visualization, imagination, extended concentration and ability to engage your emotions will be important.

The Life You Want – Get Clear

To prepare for your manifestation process, you want to get clear about what you want to manifest. Determine what type of lifestyle, career, family, social life, spiritual life and financial status you would like to create. Be specific, but also leave room for creative input from the Divine. Have a mental picture that you can regularly spend time focusing on as part of your manifestation process. Your imagination is one of the most potent tools you have. Within your imagination create scenarios of the life you want so that you can use these during meditations, walks, any time you are alone or are able to concentrate without distraction.

When it comes to money manifestation, if you are just starting out and have never attempted this before, it is wise to choose a goal that is believable by your conscious mind, but just slightly above. For instance, if you believe you can manifest $10,000 in the next 1 month to 3 months, I would up it slightly to $12,000 or $15,000. This is because it needs to be believable to your conscious mind. This enables you to be able to create the mental images and thought processes that will inform your subconscious of what you want to manifest. If you start with $1,000,000 as a goal you would probably have resistance from your conscious mind (inner critic.) It may delay the connection to your subconscious mind. Your subconscious mind has a stronger influence in the creation process. We all have preconceived beliefs and ideas about wealth and our ability to obtain it. They can hinder and probably have already hindered your goals. You need to stretch beyond limiting beliefs little by little. When you approach it this way, you are setting yourself up for success. Once you receive the financial goal you are working on, this success overwrites the previous perception in your conscious mind. It has upgraded proof of what you are capable of doing. You will have more confidence in creating bigger, more elaborate desires going forward. You want to get your conscious mind to work in support of your goals and aspirations, so that your subconscious mind can power your manifestation goals.

In your quest to manifest huge finances (i.e. lottery win, business success) or anything that allows for you to be able to have the ability to have influence in a large way, the reasons for manifesting it need to be bigger than just you – your desire for it. In order for there to be a strong magnetic pull into your reality, your reasons should be elevated in such a way that it includes the desire to help others. Whether it's your family, friends, community or some type of charity goal, when you desire to help others the energy you put out is more attractive to the frequency of abundance and prosperity.

Let's Get Started

Get out a piece of paper. Better yet, get a journal or notebook that you will use specifically to record your manifestation goals and results. That way you will be able to track your progress. Divide the book into two sections. Leave the front half of the book for your goals. The second half is for recording when your manifestation happens. Keep in mind that your manifestations may show up differently than you imagine them. Be open minded and understand that prosperity and abundance show up in many ways. For instance, I was working on a particular abundance process. I hadn't seen results just yet, but was still continuing the process. I received an email for a class action settlement which resulted in me getting 10 years worth of free product that roughly amounted to $6000. The product is something that I already own and would have continued pay for monthly to own. Now, I don't have to pay for it and the product will be mine for the next ten years. That is an unexpected prosperity manifestation. We love those!

Gratitude

Although we are working towards manifesting our desires, it is important to recognize and deeply appreciate what we have and where we are in life right now. The energy of gratitude is healing and uplifting. It makes us recognize that no matter where we are in life, we are blessed. This is an energetic state of mind that resonates a vibration that attracts more of what you are going to be grateful for. This helps your vibratory energy to resonate in such a way that is conducive for more goodness to come in. Energy attracts similar energy. Keeping a mind-set of gratitude is one of the ways that you can create more abundance. Gratitude is uplifting and positive which are conducive to prosperity and abundance.

Minding the Subconscious

We are not taught to manage or guard our subconscious mind. There are many beliefs that get programmed in that aren't necessarily helpful. It is up to us when we become aware of its importance, to manage our own subconscious so that it works for us in ways that strengthen and support our goals and desires. We want to make sure our subconscious holds beliefs and ideas about us that will help us be the best version of ourselves. Our subconscious is like a computer. It is responsible for running the background programming where all the really impactful beliefs about ourselves and our lives are held. It is important to constantly program your subconscious with ideas and beliefs about you and your life that are in support of you creating the abundant life you deserve.

An effective way to reprogram your subconscious is by using affirmations daily. Take some quiet, uninterrupted time to compile a set of affirmations that are uplifting and that counter your own negative self-limiting beliefs.

Be very honest with yourself about deep down feelings that you are harboring that are negative. Once you identify them, create a word or phrase that counters this belief. For example, "I am afraid that I won't achieve my dreams" can be countered by "I am courageous. Each day, I boldly take steps to manifest my dreams." Another way to develop affirmations is to take a subject matter such as "affirmations for courage" or "affirmations for fear" and search the internet for the affirmations to spark ideas of what to include in your list. It is important to create affirmations specifically to target the emotions and beliefs you want to change. I have affirmations for different topics such as "courage, connecting with higher self, self-worth, strength, happiness, etc." There are lots of resources online to help. Overtime as you develop in the areas you have been working on, you will need to modify and update your affirmations.

Another impactful way to reprogram your subconscious mind is self-hypnosis. This is the process by which you have a pre-recorded session that you use that addresses the various areas that you wish to reprogram. There are sources online that can act as examples. What I recommend is to listen to various different ones recorded by others and create your own using your voice. This is more powerful because it is your voice that is the one that your subconscious has been listening to all your life. If doing this doesn't appeal to you, you can purchase a pre-recorded hypnosis session from a reputable source. Using headphones or earphones will be the most effective.

Lastly, another way to reprogram the mind is to post symbols, words and phrases all around your home and workplace strategically placed so you will see them all throughout the day. This uses the subliminal program technique advertising and marketing is known for. Strong, relevant symbolism and repetitive visual engagement have a way of gradually seeping into the subconscious. The best times to have your self-hypnosis sessions are upon wakening and just before going to sleep. Your brain waves are most receptive and will transmit to your subconscious mind more easily.

The Power of Emotions

Emotions move people to do things with passion and commitment. Emotions are temporary and fleeting and we ride the wave of them until there is a change. After an emotional peak, we go back to being at our normal levels of energy. The emotions that evoke almost immediate reaction are excitement, joy, anger, sorrow and emotional pain. The energetic frequency produced during emotional episodes resonates so strongly it is almost tangible. In fact, its presence can be felt by anyone in the near vicinity of the person experiencing it. That's how powerful emotions are.

Emotions can either reinforce or derail what you are working to energetically manifest. During an emotional episode, the frequency emitted becomes part of your energetic signature until it subsides. In order to ensure that your emotions support your manifestation work, you will need to observe the following steps:

When a particularly powerful emotion shows up such as. joy, excitement, intense laughter (joyful expression) no matter what it is about, take a moment to say affirmations, script or visualize a manifestation goal. Hold on to the emotion as strongly as you can. Breathe deeply before and after to seal it in. Positive emotions are acutely aligned with the vibration of abundance and prosperity. They attract each other.

Emotional moments are fleeting. Catch the energy of them and use them to boost your manifestation work as often as you can. Keeping keenly alert and aware of the emotional flares during your period of manifestation work is important in order to capture the energy and use it to benefit what you are doing.

Subsequently, negative emotions can also be channeled to support your work, however, the method is slightly different. Negative emotions are dense. They are dissonant (out of harmony) to the energies of abundance and prosperity. Negative emotions carry us away to a point where we are not aware that we have been swept away until a short time after. Once we recognize that we are in a negative emotional state, it is very important to find a quiet place to sit and focus on what we are feeling. Breathing deeply focus inward and introduce positive thoughts and affirmations to counter the negatives ones. If you are currently prone to negative emotions, have affirmations or the words/phrases to counter them already written out to be ready to use for moments like this. Carry them with you.

While you're focused within, close your eyes and see a color the represents your feelings… red, purple, orange. It doesn't matter. Whatever comes to mind first. Visualize this color as a wave of energy that surrounds you like an outer layer in the shape of an egg. Begin to draw the energy down into a ball the size of a baseball that is hovering right in front of your stomach. This is your negative emotion contained in an energy ball. You can either disperse it out into the heavens to be transmuted into light energy, or you can take the ball of energy and focus it into your affirmations as you read them out loud with passion drawn from the energy ball. You can also turn it into a pen shape and let it help you script (discussed later in the book) your life by overlaying it on top of your writing hand with the actual pen in it. See and feel it as strong, passionate energy going into the pen then going onto the page with the words you are writing. This is a transmutation of negative energy into a useful form.

Negative Beliefs About Money

If money is one of the things you are working to manifest, it is important to identify and recognize the beliefs that you hold that may sabotage your efforts. Negative beliefs about money will hinder the manifesting process. At the onset it is important to do the work required to identify and begin to heal any blockages you may have about money and wealth.

Do you think you are worthy? Often times we harbor feelings of unworthiness. You believe that any kind of success is not something you deserve to obtain. If you have feelings like this, it is important to begin to reverse those feelings and begin to embrace your worthiness.

Do you believe money is evil? Many of us were raised with the belief that money is evil. That is not the case. Money is a means of exchange. Whether it is used negatively or not is dependent on the mindset and character of the person in question. Money and other forms of wealth are merely tools that can be exchanged for the great experiences that you will make happen in your life and the lives of your loved ones.

Do you harbor a "lack" mentality? Our experiences dictate the way we look at the world. We take in and hold on to the past as if it is your "forever future." If you were raised in an environment of lack, then it is likely that you have harbored beliefs that confirm that lack is a strong possibility for you. Even if are doing better than before, there is a constant fear that you can be thrust back into the same kind of lack.

Don't curse your bills! Do you dislike paying bills? One of the best exercises you can do to strengthen your abundance mentality is to bless your bills when they come in. Give thanks that you have them, the companies have faith that you will pay them and that you can and will pay them. Think about how good it is that you can afford to pay your bills. This is an abundance mindset. Practice it every time a bill comes in.

For a list of affirmations to help counter negative beliefs about money, go to this link: https://www.sacredmysteries.org/post/recipe-for-abundance

Your Personal Power

We are energetic beings. As energetic beings our energy emits from within out. Our personal energy resonates at a particular potency level. This level can be increased or decreased. When it comes to manifestation, increasing our energetic potency is very helpful because it is our energy that goes into everything we do, including our manifestation work. At whatever energetic level you are, it can be increased by a few simple methods.

Getting the proper amount of sleep is important to our overall health but is also important to how potent our energy is. Get plenty of rest every night to ensure your energy is at its peak. A healthy diet is also crucial to your energy. Our food is one of our energy sources. How we eat affects the quality and potency of our energy. Fresh foods over processed foods will always support a healthy body that supports the energy that we resonate. Exercising regularly also increases the potency of our personal energy. Engaging in power walking, tai chi, yoga, dance or any other form of physical activity that is healthy for the body will increase your personal energy.

Another technique to raise your personal energy is called in Hindu Sanskrit, Pranayama. It is the practice of controlling the breath. The breath is the only thing the body cannot do without for more than a few minutes or it will expire. The act of breathing is the most important for survival above all of the body's other needs. The breath, breathing air in and out, has the power of life and death. Harnessing the energy of the breath in building personal power will help to internally activate and strengthen the flow of kundalini (personal energy.) Strengthening of the flow of the energy of your personal power becomes part of your energetic signature and will automatically go towards your manifestation work.

There are breathing patterns that can be utilized to increase the flow of our personal energy. One such exercise is the Fire Breath which is deep belly rapid breaths. This breathing is a controlled breath that quickly takes air in through the nose, down into the lower belly and pushes it all the way out just as quickly. The breath in should result in filling the diaphragm with air that extends the belly all the way out. Then immediately pressing the diaphragm in to push the belly in and the air out all the way out. Then repeat for a total cycle of 24 to 32 breaths. Have an interval of four regular breaths in between each cycle. Three to five cycles should be sufficient to begin with. Make sure you are seated and sitting up with your shoulders back. After each cycle you should feel a little heat all over. This is your kundalini energy (personal divine energy) being stimulated. You may also feel a little lightheaded due to the amount of air you are taking in quickly. Stay seated to ensure you keep your balance. Stand only when the lightheaded feeling passes. Making breathing techniques a regular practice daily or a few times a week will help to increase the intensity of your personal energy.

THE TECHNIQUES

Scripting

Scripting is the method of writing out what you want. It is similar to developing a script for a play or a movie, however, you are writing out your life as you want it to be. It is a simple but powerful technique. It engages the intellect, visual, mental and motor skills in this process of manifesting. You can use a journal to write out your manifestation scripting and also to record the results.

Put aside some time to contemplate your life as you want it. Shape it into a story that you will write into your manifestation journal. Write it in the present tense. It is the subconscious that acts on the desires we want. Your subconscious mind accepts it as a truth of what needs to happen in the now of your life and works towards bringing it into being. This is way more impactful and aids in faster manifestation than if you were to write it in the future tense. Your subconscious mind has a strong effect on the resonance of your vibrational energy. What you resonate you attract. If you are able to go into an alpha or theta state of awareness (dreamlike state) while writing this will also enhance its effectiveness. A dreamlike state is where our subconscious lives and thrives and is the best state to imprint desires.

Some questions to ask yourself as you begin to create your life script:

- Where are you living?
- What is your career or business/es?
- What does your social life look like?
- Are you married with kids, or are you dating?
- Do you travel often?

- What are your daily routines that bring you joy? Walking, reading, sunbathing, swimming....
- Are you wealthy or financially free?
- What type of surroundings are you enjoying?

Write it as descriptive as you can. Unleash your creativity. This allows you to go outside of your logical mind which tends to be restrictive in what it will allow. Treat your writing like an autobiography that someone else is going to read, with all the juicy bits. Include colors, textures and scents and sound. A few times per week, read your story out loud. Saturate yourself in the vision and emotion of it all. As you're reading it, lose yourself into it. Then release any attachment to the outcome.

You can script on a daily, weekly or monthly basis for manifestations such as a new job, a new living space, equipment, a new car, travel, to bring about beneficial circumstances, personal growth, etc. Remember, to write it in the present tense.

Visualization

The mind is where creation is born. Anything that is manifested must first be a thought. The Divine Creator creates all of reality out of its Divine Mind. We are a reflection of the Divine Creator. On a lessor level, we create our reality out of our minds. Anything that you have ever done in life began with a thought and seeing it in your "mind's eye." We do this instinctively. Now it is time to take this instinct and direct it for your personal manifestation goals.

When we are children we are gifted at visualization. We spend hours either daydreaming or imagining all kinds of things. I remember when I was a child, I could consciously control my dreams. If I liked a particular dream, I would continue it the next night. My imagination was very active. I would spend hours in an imaginary world. We all have done this as children. Being able to regain our childlike ability to travel into the vivid realm of our imagination is indispensable in this work. It is important to understand that our imaginations are powerful tools. Mentally, we are sending the images of the story of the current state of our lives over and over again to our subconscious. As a result, we are reliving everything over and over again. Using creative visualization, you can send a new version of the life that you want to manifest.

If your ability to visualize in clear pictures is strong, create a scenario of the life that you want. See it clearly, with depth and color. Bring in sounds and smells if you can. Make it as real as possible. It is important to do this regularly. Setup a schedule. It only takes several minutes at a time. If your ability to visualize is not as strong, begin to practice visualization by taking an object, looking at it and taking in all of its details. Then close your eyes and recreate it in your mind. Repeat this over and over until you have formed it in your mind in detail. Gradually, expand to practice on visualizing whole sections of rooms, areas in nature or areas in your neighborhood. Once you have developed your visualization techniques you are ready to give great depth and detail to your manifestation visualization. However, don't wait to start visualizing your manifestation goals. You can start visualizing and then begin to sharpen and deepen your visualization as you progress in your practicing.

Consistency is important as you are building up and amplifying the resonating energy of what you want to manifest in order to not only attract it, but to be aware of opportunities, synchronicities and inspirations that come to you. Often times, we miss opportunities because of where we are mentally and emotionally. Visualization helps us keep our goals and dreams at the forefront of our priorities. We then become keenly aware of any and all opportunities that can help us make our dreams come true and to act upon those opportunities and/or inspirations that come. A regular visualization schedule will be helpful. It will only take a few minutes at a time and will add valuable and necessary energy to your manifestation goals.

Act as If

This process of manifestation encompasses all of the laws of abundance. The law of abundance's core tool is attraction/magnetism. A very potent way of increasing attraction/magnetism of what you are manifesting is to "act as if."

You see, the version of yourself you wish to manifest already exists on a vibratory level in another reality. Through focus and practice you will be able to connect within and bring it through to your present reality. In order to bring it through into your current reality you have to lock into its vibratory rate.

"Acting as if" is a method through which you can connect to the vibratory rate (frequency) of the version of your life that you want. Use your consciousness by way of visualization to define and playout the version of your life that you want in such a way that you begin to vibrate at the same frequency as what you desire. This requires a clear mental picture of the life you want. <u>Visualize and concentrate your thoughts as if you are having it right now</u>. Think of how this lifestyle makes you feel when you wake up in the mornings and go to sleep at night. What are you feeling? Satisfaction? Ease? Comfort? Accomplished? Safe? Joyful? Excited? Imagine how you spend your days, who you hang out with, what types of activities you are involved in. What books are you reading? What is your favorite room in your house? Include all of what makes you happy. Imagine in technicolor what it all looks like. Imagine all of the emotions that you are having living this life. Feel them deep down in your body. Incorporate all of it in every way possible. In doing so, you will resonate at the vibration of your life as you intend it to be bringing it closer and closer until it fully drops into your current reality. Things will begin to align. Synchronicities will appear. People, circumstances, opportunities, offers, out of the ordinary blessings will show up like never before supporting your manifestation. You will mentality and emotionally be ready to recognize and move on whatever opportunities the Universe opens up in front of you.

Your current reality is a mirror reflection of your internal reality. By practicing "acting as if," you are resonating at the vibratory level of the life you what you want to manifest. This is a powerful way of magnetizing your energy field to align and attract it and to bring that version of your life from one reality to this one. You are dialing into the frequency that you want to bring into your current reality. Spend time doing this as often as you can. Repetitive, concentrated thought from your conscious mind will trigger your subconscious mind to prove it. To manifest it. Using this technique daily, for 10-15 minutes is recommended. This is where you will need to exercise your ability to concentrate for extended periods of time. Use your intuition to determine when you have completed each "act as if" manifestation session. You will instinctively feel and know that you have achieved the rate of resonance necessary to connect deeply with the version of life you are envisioning. When this happens, you can gently come out of the session. You can journal about your experience.

Your subconscious mind does not discriminate regarding the good or bad benefits of thoughts that are imprinted. By regularly and consistently introducing what you want by "acting as if," the subconscious mind determines it as important and take measures to create/manifest it.

To make this session go smoothly, make a recording of yourself speaking about the life that you are manifesting in advance to use as a guided meditation. Having it prerecorded will allow you to relax into it. This will help you setup the mental picture more clearly. Pour all details you can into the meditation. A clear mental picture is an important component to this technique.

The version of yourself that already exists in another reality is waiting there for you. In order to bring it through into your current reality you have to lock into the vibratory frequency of it. In the same manner we dial into a particular radio station's frequency to get a particular station, you will need to dial in to the frequency of your desired life by "acting as if." This technique bypasses your critical conscious mind that sets limitations on what you are able to achieve and connects with your subconscious mind to imprint your desires. The subconscious mind activates the unmanifested potentiality (formless substance/primordial force) to manifest what it has received as a prioritized command/imprint from you.

Water Manifestation

Water is one of the most prevalent and powerful elements on the entire planet. Without it, there would be no life. Water can be soft and yielding, or forceful and destructive. Mostly, water is pliable. It takes the various shapes of what it is contained in. It flows around its obstacles making its way to where it is called. It is scientifically proven that water is a conductor. The work of Dr. Masaru Emoto documented in his book, The Hidden Messages of Water, how water exposed to loving, benevolent, and compassionate human intention results in aesthetically pleasing physical molecular formations in the water while water exposed to fearful and discordant human intentions results in disconnected, disfigured, and "unpleasant" physical molecular formations.

Link to study: https://thewellnessenterprise.com/emoto/

Subsequently, we can infuse water with our intentions, manifestation goals and desires. Take a 16 to 24 oz glass bottle or jar and fill with the cleanest water you have. Oxygenated water is great, but spring or distilled will do. Go into a trance state while holding the bottle of water and begin to speak all of your desires into the water. Sip on it daily to take in what you have placed in it by the power of your words, emotions and energy. By taking in the infused manifestation water, it amplifies your energetic vibrations and aids in magnetizing your desires to you. Repeat until your intentions are manifested. I, personally, like to make it a small ritual by sitting at my altar and lighting a white (or any color of your choosing) candle while I'm infusing the water with my intentions. I pray first to get into a meditative (theta) state which is the state where our minds can communicate our desires to the creative force.

Meditation

Meditation is a method through which you train your mind to be in control of your thoughts. Meditation conditions you to disengage from the constant mental chatter going on in your mind. You learn to be a witness to your thoughts and recognize that your thoughts are not you. Meditation allows you to practice disengaging with your thoughts. This allows for a deeper connection to your Higher Self. Your Divine Self. It is also great practice for developing the ability to concentrate for extended periods of time. Extended concentration is essential in manifestation work. If you already have a meditation practice, this is great. If not, it is a good time to develop one. It is an invaluable tool for all of your spiritual and manifestation endeavors.

Mindset

It is important to maintain a positive, uplifting attitude when energetically working on manifesting a life that is resonating at a higher vibration. Negative thoughts and actions work to cancel the momentum that is being built up and undermines the manifestation process. Worry, doubt, fear, depression, anger, etc. are all contrary to the work you are doing to uplift your life. We are human so we can't always avoid these feelings.

However, as a Manifestor you must guard against engaging in these emotions for the duration of your abundance work. It is important to work towards minimizing these emotions as much as possible. They aren't healthy to the life you have now and the life you are creating. When they show up for you, process through them as quickly as you can and then properly transmute these emotions into energies that will support positivity and growth.

To transmute the negative emotional energy, take a crystal (smoky quartz, obsidian, onyx, black tourmaline) and hold it during the emotional phase. Breath in deeply and out to relax as much as possible. Visualize the crystal's healing energies going from your hands, up your arms and then spread all the way up to your head and down to your toes. At the same time visualize your negative emotion being drawn out of you into the crystal. Hold this vision for several minutes or until the emotion starts to subside. When you're finished, make sure you immerse the crystal in a bowl of sea salt and water to cleanse and rejuvenate it. You can thank the crystal for its service.

Similarly, your circle of people is also very important to your mindset. People who are constantly complaining, gossiping, spewing negativity, depressed and down on life, etc. will affect your manifestation work if you are around them consistently. Minimize interaction with people like this. When you are around them do not engage in these negative behaviors with them. Bow out of the conversation or graciously change the subject. You can choose to check-in on them periodically and love them from afar.

Surround yourself with people who are also moving towards creating a better life, who are positive and uplifting. That will support the work you are doing. You can help each other stay positive. Abundance is drawn to positivity.

Moon Phases

We are spiritually and physically influenced by the moon. The moon's phases throughout the month emit varying lunar energies over the planet that affects us and all of life. Each phase is conducive to manifestation work. The most influential moon phase for manifestation work is the Full Moon. This is a time for nurturing, passion, healing, strength and power. It is also a good time to identify and dispel negative emotions (shadow work) and is a good time to embark on healing your relationship with money and your feelings of worthiness. The New Moon energy is also a great time to initiate manifestation work or any new projects. The energy is conducive to supporting new endeavors of any kind such as: starting a new business, new beginnings of any kind, new love and romance, health or job hunting.

You can plan your manifestation projects during the appropriate moon phase to have the lunar energy supporting what you are doing. This is a great technique, but not so necessary as to inhibit the timing of when you wish to start. Start when you are ready.

Spiritual Tradition / Spirituality

Manifestation work can also be greatly enhanced by including elements of your own spiritual tradition. Connecting with the Divine in its many aspects will anoint your work with favor. Whether it includes reading bible passages, psalms, sacred texts, prayers from other traditions and offerings to the different spiritual elemental powers known by different names in various traditions, any of it will elevate your manifestation work. Your spirit guides, ancestors and other elevated spirits want you to progress and will fortify and boost the potency of your requests and manifestation work on the spiritual plane. They will also support your manifesting work by giving you guidance and insight through dreams and inspirations. This is a big part of my manifestation work. Don't hesitate to also include your own intuition in this process. Be creative! You're a creator! You are a manifestor!

Manifestation Altar

Making a manifestation (abundance/prosperity) altar will give you a sacred space to honor and focus all of your manifestation work. Find an area in your home that has relatively low traffic where you will be able to sit quietly. Place a table there or use the floor. Cover with a white or decorative cloth. Place items on it that represent your spirituality. Be sure to include representations of the 4 elements (earth, water, fire, air).

Examples of things to represent the elements are for fire use a candle; for earth, use a bowl of earth or a stone or wood; for water either a glass of water or a water symbol; and, for air, a feather or incense. You can also add things such as a dream board, symbols of abundance and prosperity (money, coins, shells, statues). Start off by smudging the area with incense or energetically cleanse by sprinkling Florida or Kananga Water, Holy Water or some other spiritual water of your choosing. Arrange the items you have selected on your altar, so it is pleasing to your eye and feels "right." Consecrate the area with prayers and affirmations. Use this area to do all of your manifestation work. By doing this, you are creating an energetic portal for your manifestation work to be concentrated and strengthened.

Manifestation Rituals

The practice of ritual is ancient. It is part of every spiritual culture and religion across the world. Ritual helps us connect with the Divine through creating a sacred container where everything that is spoken and performed is focused on a particular spiritual goal. Rituals are governed by a planned set of activities done within a certain amount of time. A ritual focuses on invoking an aspect of the Divine to enhance and deepen the presence of this aspect in our everyday lives. The ritual is a conduit that roots us into the depth of the Divine aspect we are calling upon. Performing a personal manifestation ritual can be done alone or with others. There are literally dozens of different rituals that are specific to creating abundance.

I, personally, love ritual. It is a beautiful, peaceful and spiritually creative way to connect with specific divine energies. It incorporates all of the five senses in celebration and reverence of the Divine Creator. Ritual allows for the transcendence of space and time to bring your internal realm, the spiritual realm and the physical realm together in harmony for a divine purpose.

A simple abundance ritual can be done during the New Moon of the month to be in harmony with the energy of new beginnings, especially if you are just starting your manifestation work. The ritual is to be done at home, hopefully, in front of your Abundance Altar. You will need the following:
- Green Candle (4" to 6" taper), can use white
- Incense (cinnamon, Sandalwood or rose)
- Prayer to Open the ritual
- Prosperity/Abundance Affirmations
- Abundance Prayer (in addition or in lieu of affirmations)
- Symbol of Money or Prosperity (can be a dollar bill or something else with an exchange value, or a statue of something that is representative of abundance and prosperity)
- Prayer to Close the ritual

Prepare yourself by sitting quietly in front of your altar. Do a couple of rounds of deep breathing to relax. Close your eyes and turn your attention within. After a couple of minutes, light the candle, light the incense (observe fire safety rules when lighting candle and incense.) Give thanks to the Creator and call on your guides, ancestors and angels to bless the ritual you are about to do. Ask for their loving guidance and to surround you with a circle of energetic protection. When you feel ready, read your opening prayer, then read your affirmations and prayers for manifestation. Use your intuition to add anything else that you feel called to include. Continue by performing a visualization of your abundant and prosperous life. You can even read from your Manifestation Journal or do your scripting. When you're finished, recite your closing prayer. Give thanks to the Creator and your spiritual guides and ancestors. Put out your candle.

Know that you've connected with the abundance energies and expect your manifestation to happen.

Word to the Wise

Here are some huge keys to ensure the success of your manifestations:

- Once you use any of these tools, you must maintain a "knowingness" that what you have put in motion will happen. Be patient. Stay positive. Stay the course. Manifestation takes whatever time it takes. Don't get discouraged if things don't show up in the time the you expected.

- Negativity will delay or cancel what you have put into motion. If canceled, you will have to start from scratch.

- Always be in a state of constant improvement and growth. When opportunities for advancement show up, you want to be ready and able to take full advantage.

- Repetition of these techniques is encouraged because it adds strength to the momentum of what you have put in motion. You are developing a relationship with the energy of abundance and prosperity. You are also connecting with your subconscious by repetition of your desires. It takes the time build a strong connection.

- What may be a bit tricky for some is that you also have to release attachment to the outcomes. Worry, doubt, eagerness, obsessing, over thinking, anxious anticipation will only derail your efforts. They are strong emotions that are attached to your past experiences. They have no place in your current situation. It communicates to the Universe that you do not believe what you have desired will manifest. The Universe will respond in kind. Keeping a healthy balance of stoicism and positivity will go far in supporting your manifestation endeavors.

Harm None

These manifestation techniques are to be used for your life and to influence and shape your life condition. They should not be used to exert your will over anyone else. Another important note is that there is a rule of "harm none." Your manifestation goals should not include anything that is to bring harm or take anything away from anyone else. Behaving in this way is not only incorrect, but will also undermine your prosperity work because you're engaging in "lack mentality." Even if you feel you are completely in the right to take something from someone, let it be handled by the spiritual law of reciprocity. If it comes back to you, then good. If not, something else even better will come to you. Let it go.

Recap

What you desire already exists in the astral realm as potential. What manifestation techniques help you do is to activate this version and bring it into the present into your reality. The information in this book is an entry into basic manifestation techniques that are easy and accessible. These techniques, if used properly, will help you manifest your best life. We've touched on several areas that you can do all on your own. Self-determination and spiritual sovereignty means that you own your spiritual journey and invoke dominion over your present and your future. You can create the life you envision for yourself using your intention, visualization, personal power, commitment and consistency.

Summary

The most important element in all of this, is you. You are the powering agent that fuels everything. Your intentions, mindset, dedication, personal power and consistency are the most powerful ingredients to manifesting whatever it is you want in life.

Manifesting is a creative endeavor that is fortified by your emotions, imagination, dedication, consistency in order to fully work. The techniques described in this book are skillful ways to harness and direct all of these areas to laser focus on your goals and desires. This focus is essential in manifestation. Additionally, when you also enlist the support and input of your Spirit Team (ancestors, spirit guides, angels, etc.) this forms a powerful combination that results in manifestation after manifestation.

Engaging in the art of manifestation is a spiritual practice as it requires you to delve within and assess and realign your energy in ways that connects you to your Higher Self and your purpose. We become more selective in the types of thoughts we engage in knowing that they can influence our current reality. We gain a little more understanding and a deep appreciation of the creative energy that goes into bringing things into being. We take less for granted, as our sense of gratitude is also elevated. We begin to acutely understand who we are as spiritual and energetic manifestations of God. When we are manifesting, we are mirroring in a very small way how the Divine creates. This stimulates an even deeper reverence for life and our Creator.

Recommendations... Focus, focus, focus

In any energetic endeavor it is important to stay focused. Not one day should go by that you have not engaged in your manifestation techniques. The building of a momentum of energy directed towards manifesting your goals is what is at work when you are consistent and focused. When your thoughts, energy, emotions and actions are organized behind your desires in a consistent and repetitive cycle, you can create what you want.

What is also important is to keep the details of your manifestation work out of regular conversations. What you don't want to do is to sabotage your work by inviting comments and opinions of others that may affect your mindset and attitude. Share with people who understand this realm of energy work. Once something has manifested, then discuss it as much as you like.

Once you begin your manifestation techniques, it is important to pay close attention to your intuition. Your Higher Self, that essence of you that stays connected to the Divine, will communicate important guidance through your intuition. It will probably become more active during this time.

Gratitude, again...

Although we talked about gratitude previously, I cannot emphasize enough the importance of gratitude. Putting manifestation goals aside, gratitude is an extremely positive attitude and emotion. It signals to the Universe and your subconscious that you already know that you are blessed and abundant without the material appearance of it. If you don't appreciate what you have now, very likely that you will not fully appreciate when you have more. Without true gratitude there will be an insatiable appetite for the acquisition of things that we believe will satisfy us and provide us with ongoing pleasure. This is far from the truth. Gratification with things is temporary. Of course, when you first get a desired thing, you feel happy about it. However, that feeling (like all) fades and then your mind will focus on something else to acquire that promises to satisfy you. The only true satisfaction is gratitude. The only true and lasting happiness comes from within, your connection to the Divine.

Words of Encouragement

You are a brave soul who knows your worth. By reading this book you have taken a step towards owning your right to manifest the life you deserve. Always stay the course when achieving your dreams. This life is about both the inner and outer experience. Manifestation work will make you look at yourself in many different ways. It will challenge you to think and expand your reach in new ways. It will support you stepping boldly into the best version of yourself and the best life that you are able to give yourself. This path of manifestation is a brave undertaking where the payoff is achieving your aspirations. Embarking on this path will also require that you do the internal work to know who you are and what you want in life. Doing manifestation work takes you on a journey through your spiritual and mental inner landscapes to more fully understand who you are as both a spiritual and mental being. That's the juicy part.

Closing

In truth, what people really want are to live joyously, to be surrounded by loving relationships, to feel perpetual happiness and pleasantness within, to be in harmonious and peaceful day to day environments, and to feel connected to community and to something greater than themselves. Regardless of the things you want to manifest, the most important manifestation is a state of internal happiness, a state of happiness that requires nothing external in order to exist.

I trust that the information in this book will help you manifest your desires. They have helped me and many others.

Special Thanks

This work would not be complete without mentioning the unending support and encouragement by some very special people in my life. First, my daughter, Tehja A. Fagains, whose vision of me I continue to hold and strive towards. She is my rock and my biggest encourager. She inspires me and is the reason I continue to move forward on my path. Her faith in my work keeps me grounded and on course. She also designed the photoshoot for the cover, took the photos and did an amazing makeup look! My big sister, Denise Phillips, who is always there to cheer me on, support me and she also helped me edit this work. She is one of the people I look up to most! A brilliant mind, extraordinary woman and a sweet spirit. My other big sister, Yvette Jackson, who is a light and love that is always there to nurture and lift me up. She reminds me of the beauty that resides within. I am also supremely thankful for the love and support of my spiritual sisterhood that surrounds me—Kathleen Bullock, Gladys Wrenick and Amy Fabrikant, whom I can always count on for love, advice and insight. Last but certainly not least, my coach and mentor, Abiola Abrams, who continuously guides, inspires and challenges me to discover my best self and to translate that part of me to those whose lives I touch. The wisdom and knowledge that she gives is drenched in love and inspiration.

About the Author

Rev. Mignon Grayson is the Founder of Sacred Mysteries World Wide and an ordained Interspiritual Indigenous Faith Minister of One Spirit Interfaith Seminary in New York City. She was ordained in 2016. She chose the interfaith path due to her calling to serve people of all faiths and religious practices. Mignon recognizes that there is a common link to the Divine Creator within all religious traditions.

She is a devotee of the Ifa Orisha tradition of Nigeria and initiated as a Yayi (Priestess) in Palo Mayombe, rooted in Congo spiritual traditions. As a result of her spiritual journey, Mignon has learned the deep importance of the ancestors and their connection to daily life and spiritual evolution. Ancestral reverence is an inherent core practice throughout most ancient cultures. Mignon's particular focus is to bring the wisdom of ancient spiritual traditions from across the world to the masses through Sacred Mysteries World Wide with classes, lectures, symposiums and creating on-going conversations about spirituality and its primary importance in evolving and healing the planet.

As a spiritual evolutionary coach, Mignon seeks to inspire and support people on their spiritual journey by assisting them in connecting with their most authentic and sacred soul expression. As a sound healer, Mignon uses the vibrational energies of sound to bring about healing by energy recalibration. She works passionately to be a constant vessel of healing, love and spirituality.

To leave a review of this book on Amazon:

https://www.amazon.com/dp/B07ZZLS5ST

Other Books by the Author:

The Art of Manifestation:
Rituals, Crystals, Herbs, Oils & Baths to Create the
Abundant Life You Deserve

Stay connected! Sign Up for our Blog.
www.sacredmysteries.org/signup

Links

rev_mignon@sacredmysteries.org

Follow us on Instagram @sacredmysteries_ww

Checkout the blog at our website: www.sacredmysteries.org/blog

Facebook: Sacred Mysteries Worldwide

YouTube Channel: Sacred Mysteries World Wide

———

We Are Always Here to Help!

Just getting started on your spiritual path? Click the links below to our YouTube channel which has videos that can help you on your journey:

Sacred Mysteries World Wide YouTube Channel:

https://www.youtube.com/channel/UCpgEudpK0Rhs3KaPii7ZIaw

Cont'd – links to Youtube videos:

"Tips for Beginning on A Spiritual Path"
https://youtu.be/KoxmNyaIxLg

"Getting Started Meditating – The Basics"
https://youtu.be/AtY_a4gCdBY

"Beginning Meditation 2 – Chanting"
https://youtu.be/j2wDKmFROVs

"Ancestors: How to Honor, Connect & Setup an Altar"
https://youtu.be/PKKxv8-h3JY

"How to Create an Ancestor Altar *Simple*"
https://youtu.be/IVWJI7HQMBc

Printed in Great Britain
by Amazon

66266518R00028